CR
Sto

FRIENDS
OF ACPL

Y0-BJO-032

New Wheels

Copyright © 1978, Raintree Publishers Limited

All rights reserved. No part of this book may be reproduced or utilized in any form or by any means, electronic or mechanical, including photocopying, recording, or by any information storage and retrieval system, without permission in writing from the Publisher. Inquiries should be addressed to Raintree Publishers Limited, 205 West Highland Avenue, Milwaukee, Wisconsin 53203.

Library of Congress Number: 77-27052

1 2 3 4 5 6 7 8 9 0 82 81 80 79 78

Printed in the United States of America.

Library of Congress Cataloging in Publication Data

McLenighan, Valjean.
 New wheels.

 SUMMARY: A confrontation occurs between two friends when one discovers that the other has stolen from a local store.
 [1. Stealing—Fiction] I. Gubin, Mark. II. Title.
PZ7.M22492Ne   [E]   77-27052
ISBN 0-8172-1152-7 lib. bdg.

New Wheels

Words by Valjean McLenighan

Pictures by Mark Gubin

Childrens Press

© 1978, Raintree Publishers Limited.

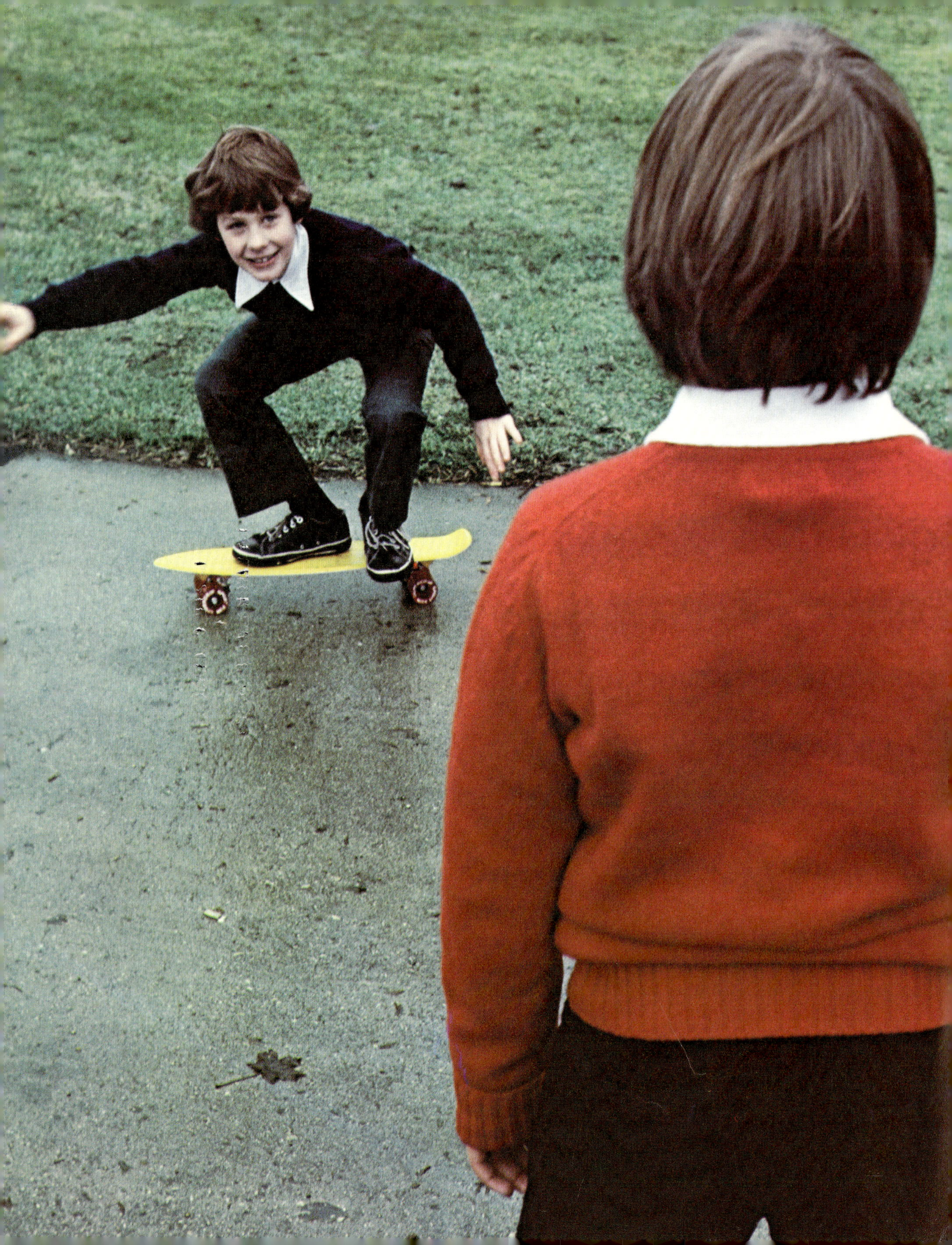

I got to know Barry when he moved in next door. The first time I saw him on a skateboard, I knew he was great.

He can do kick turns, 360s, you name it. Nobody's faster at downhilling.

I'm afraid to go that fast. But Barry's always saying things like, "You have to take chances if you want to get places."

At first I thought he talked like that from watching TV. But then I found out he really believes it.

You can tell by the way he skateboards. He just doesn't get scared. And that's not all. He's always thinking up good stuff to do.

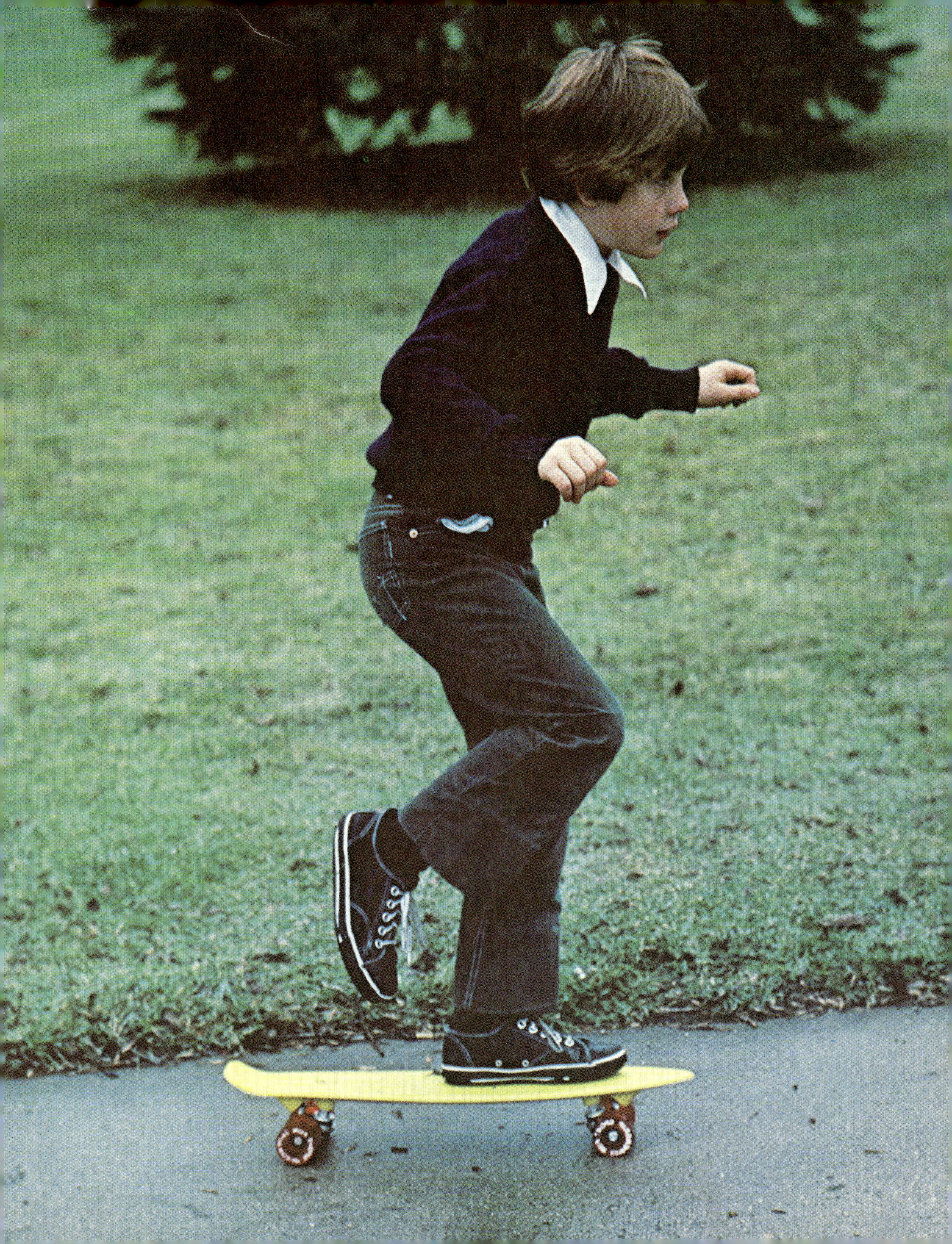

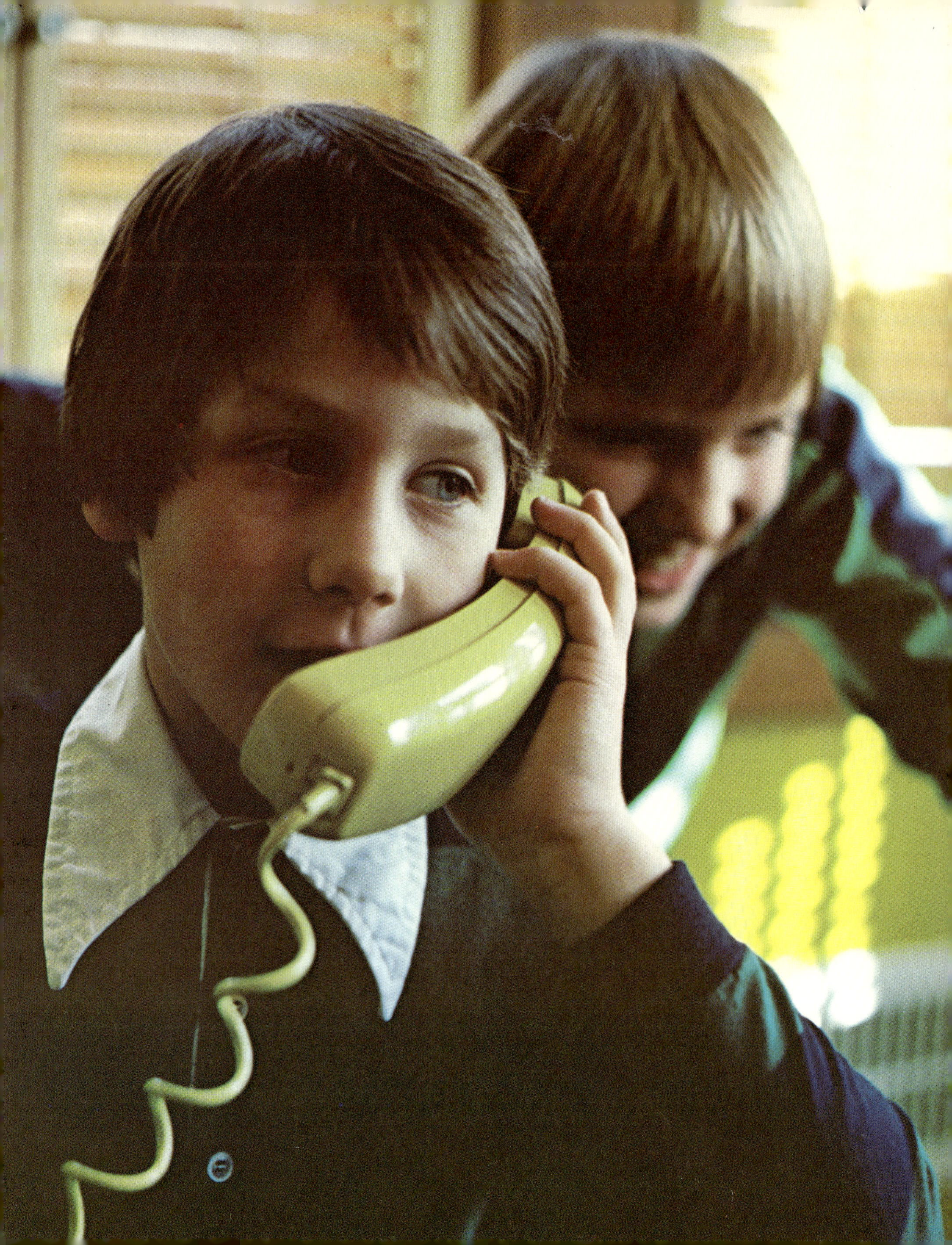

Like the time we made all those phone calls. Barry was staying over at my house. Mom and Dad were downstairs. Barry got a number out of the phone book.

Every fifteen minutes he called it and asked for Tom. After three or four calls, the people started getting mad. So Barry made one last call. He said, "This is Tom. Were there any calls for me?"

What a scream. I knew it wasn't right. My mom hates getting phone calls from people selling magazines and stuff. She would have been pretty mad if she'd caught us. But we weren't really hurting anyone. And besides, it sure was fun.

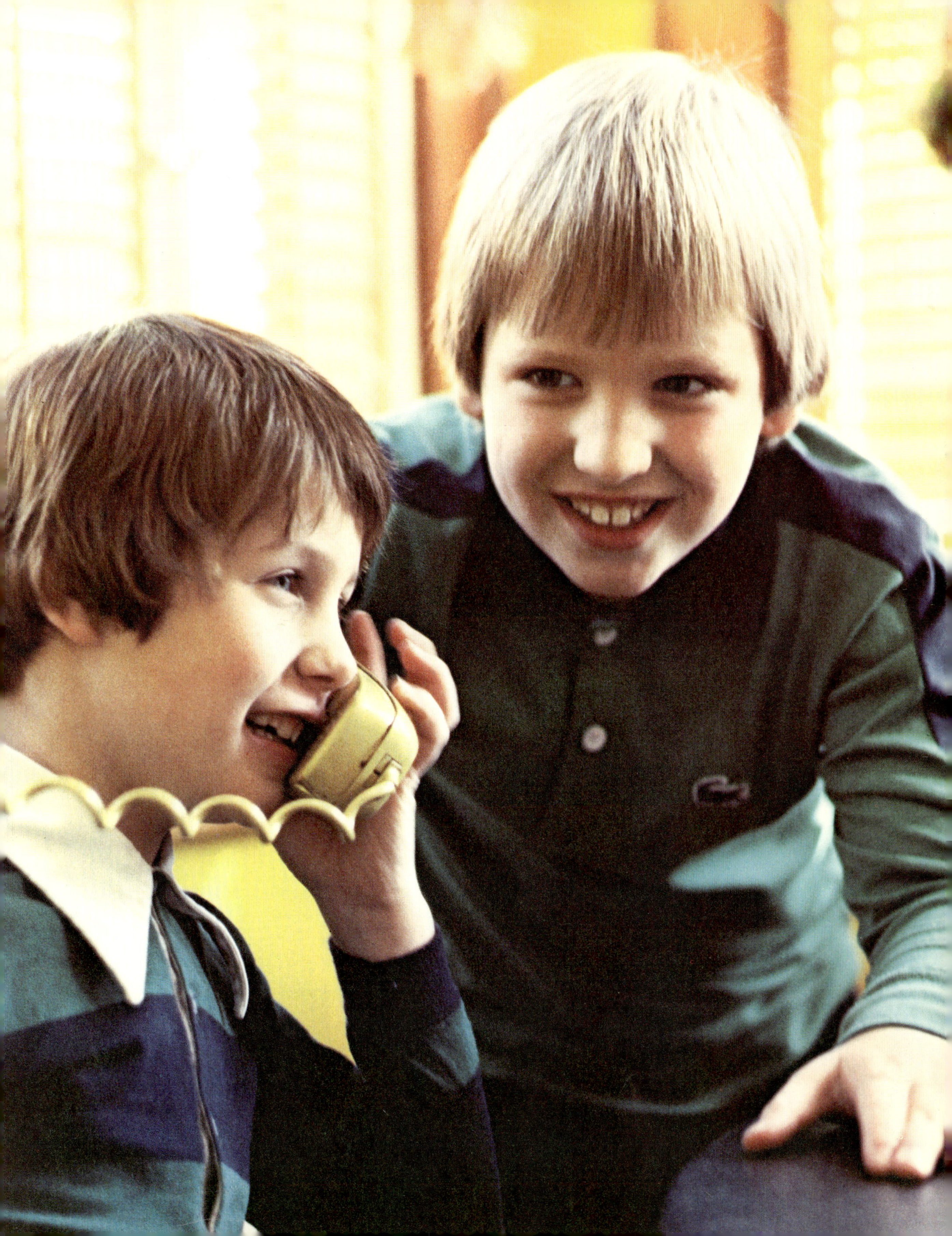

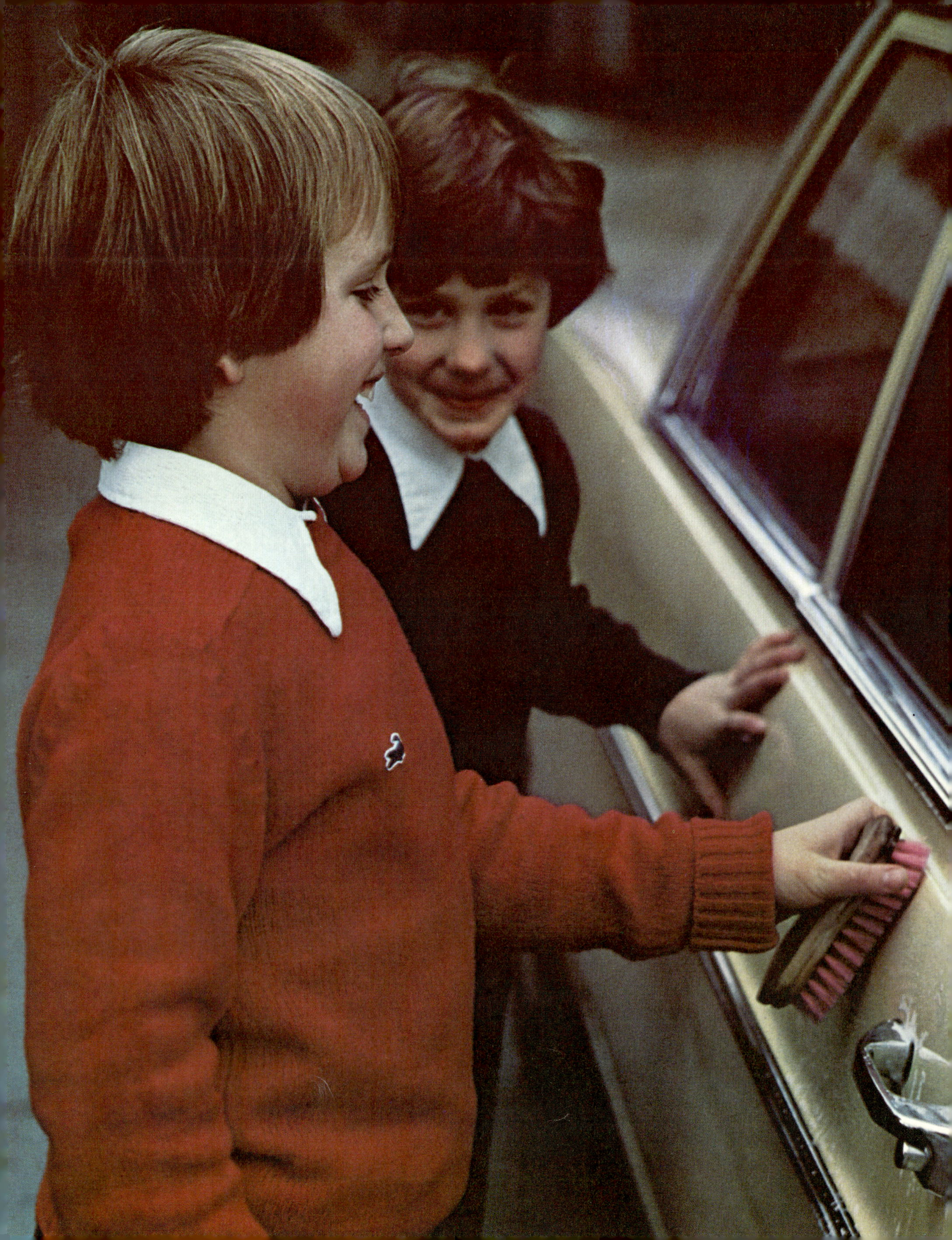

Barry and I have been spending a lot of time together lately. He's been showing me tricks on the skateboard. He even helped me wash the car last week. See, I've been trying to earn money for new skateboard wheels. I'm even thinking of getting a paper route. But Barry keeps saying that's doing it the hard way.

Barry came over after school today. He handed me this brown paper bag.

"Here's something to make your life a little easier," he said.

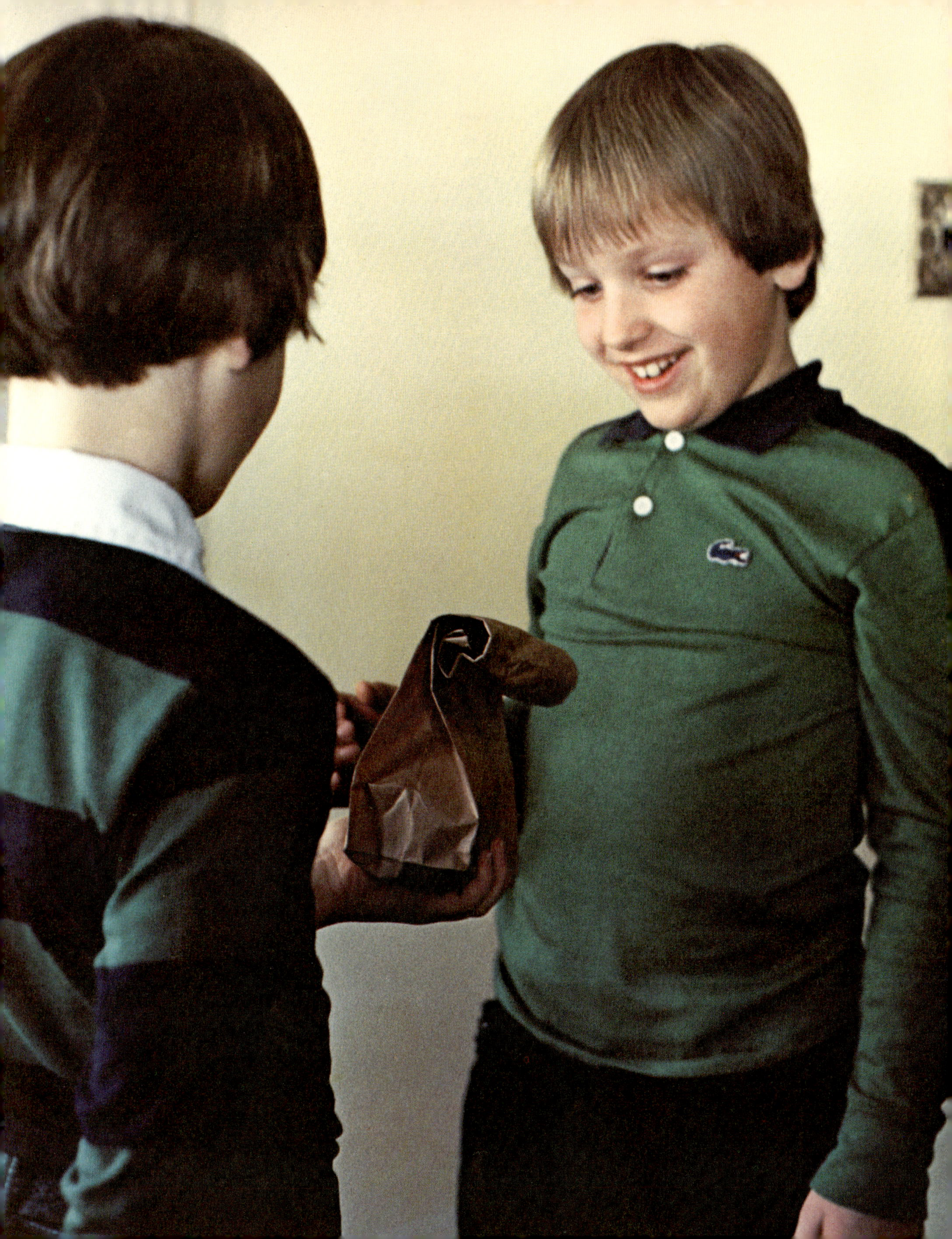

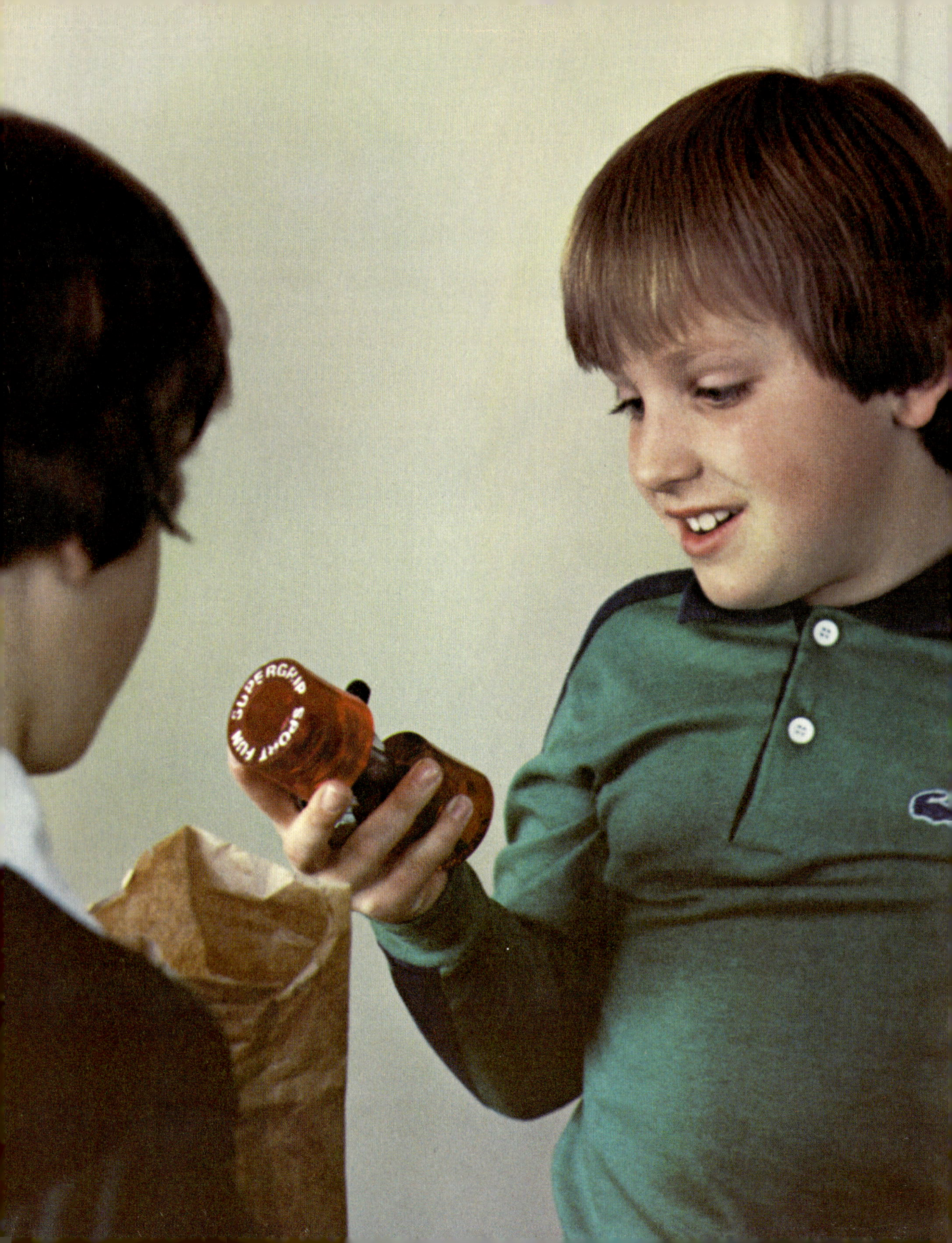
SUPERGRIP
SPORT FUN

Inside was a brand new set of skateboard wheels.

"Oh, wow!" I said. "How did you get these?"

"Nothing to it," he said. "There was a whole table full at Gordon's Sports. Nobody was around. So I put them in my jacket."

"You mean you just took them?" I asked. I couldn't believe it.

"Sure," he said. "There were lots of wheels on that table. They'll never even know these are gone."

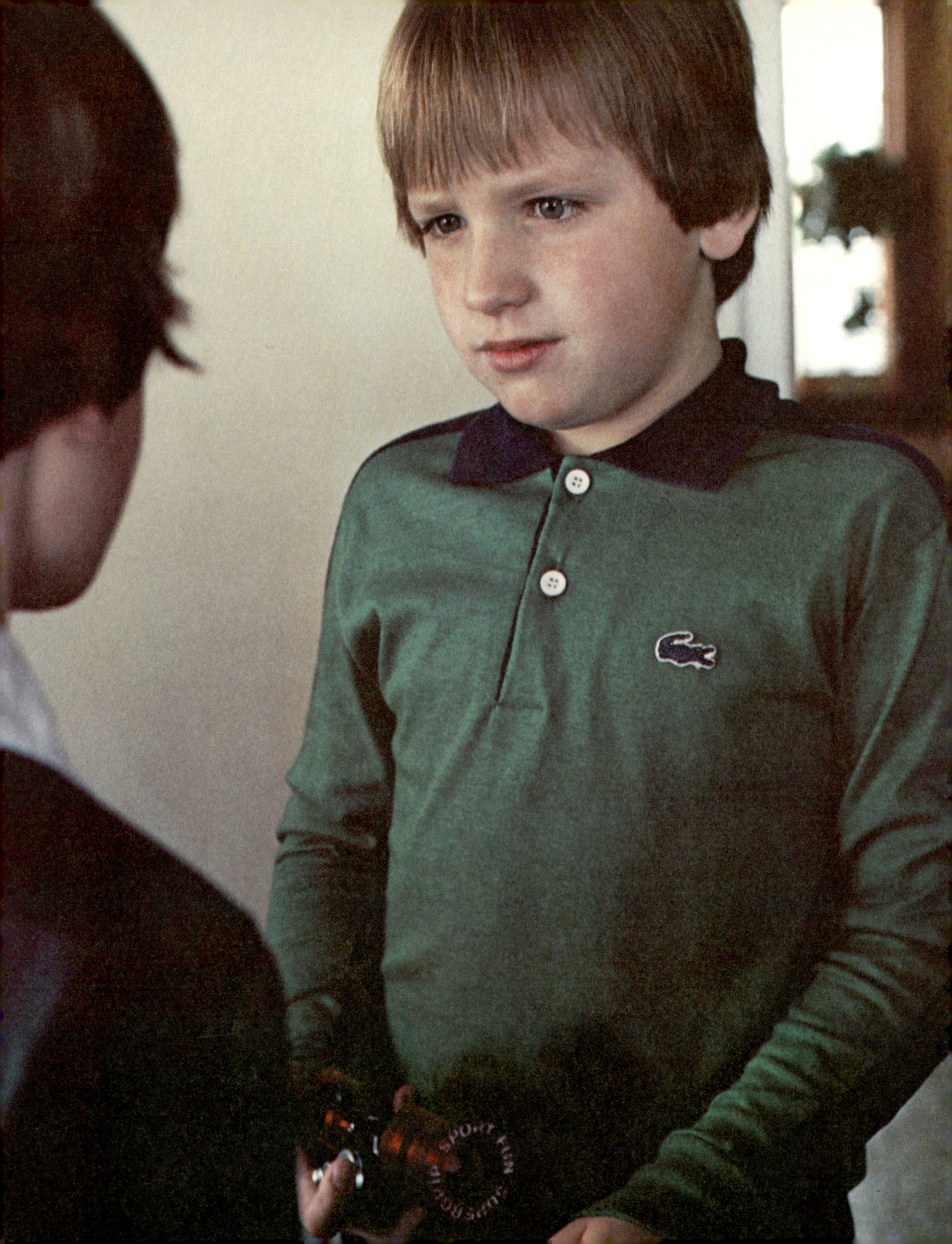

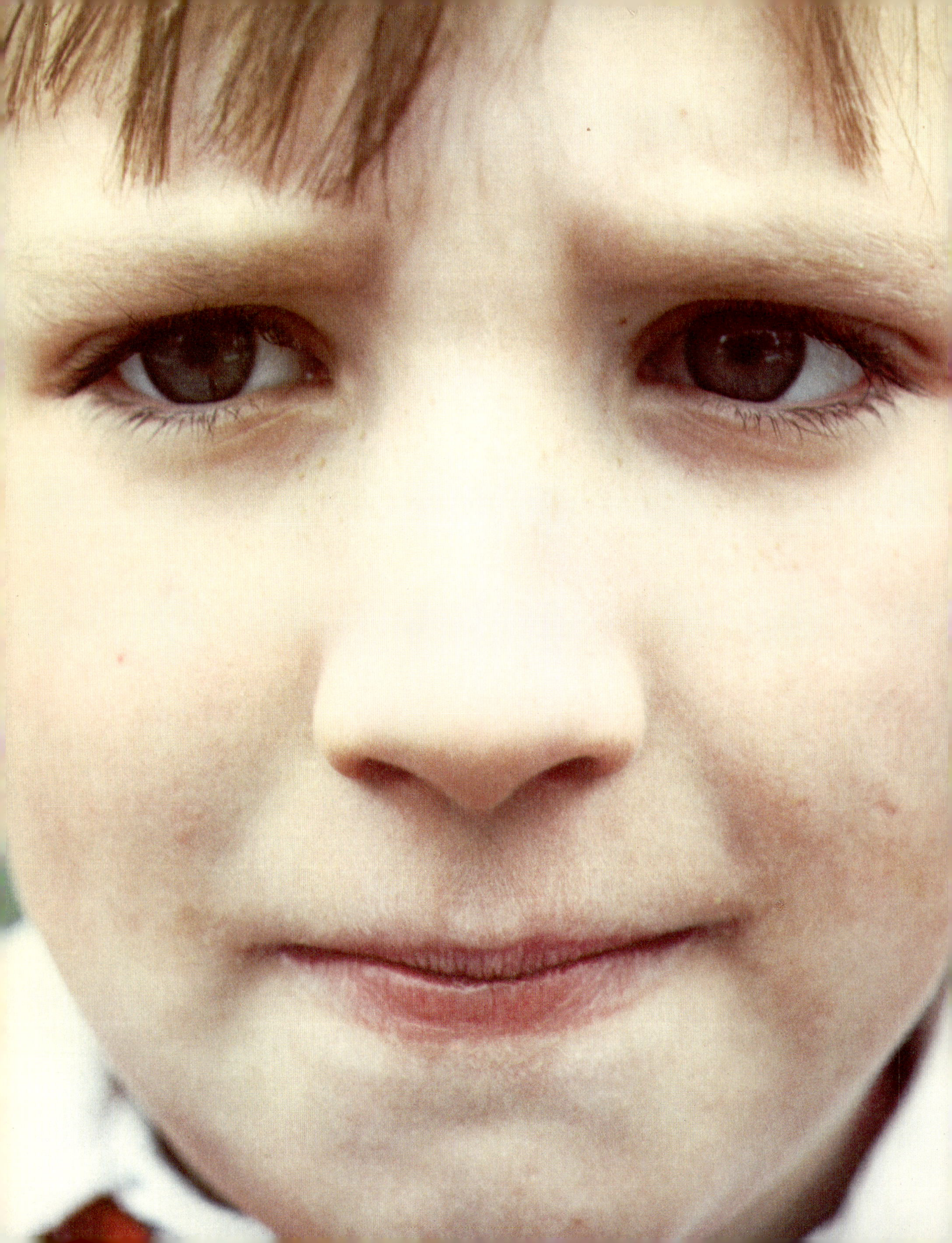

"I don't want them, Barry," I said. "I feel funny about it."

"Oh, come on," Barry said. "It was just a game."

"It was not," I said. "It was stealing."

"Well, so what?" Barry said. "I'm the one who took them, not you."

I didn't know what to say. I guess I just looked at him.

"Boy," he said. "I try to do something nice for a friend, and look what happens. Well, I don't need new wheels. You do what you want with them. I'm going home."

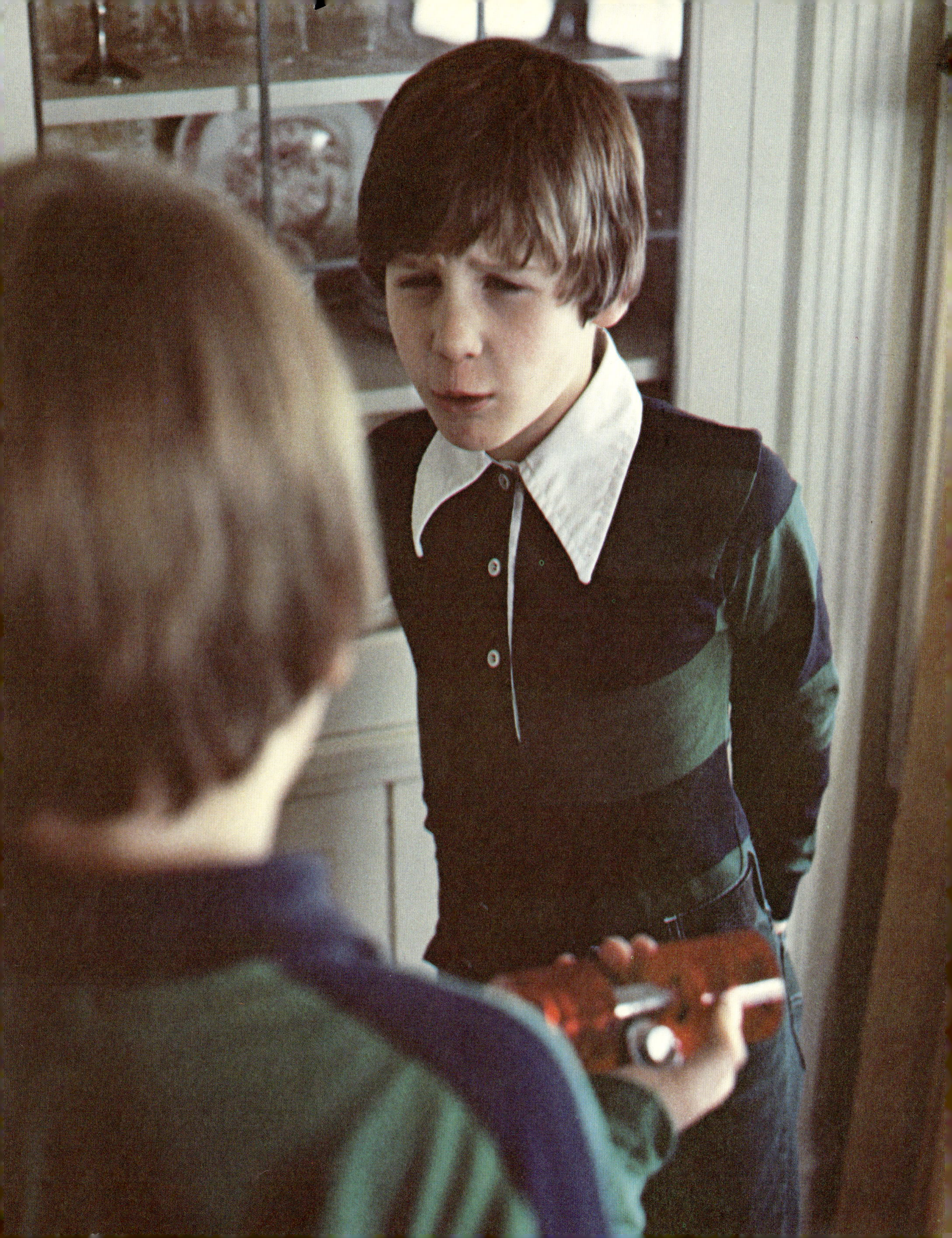

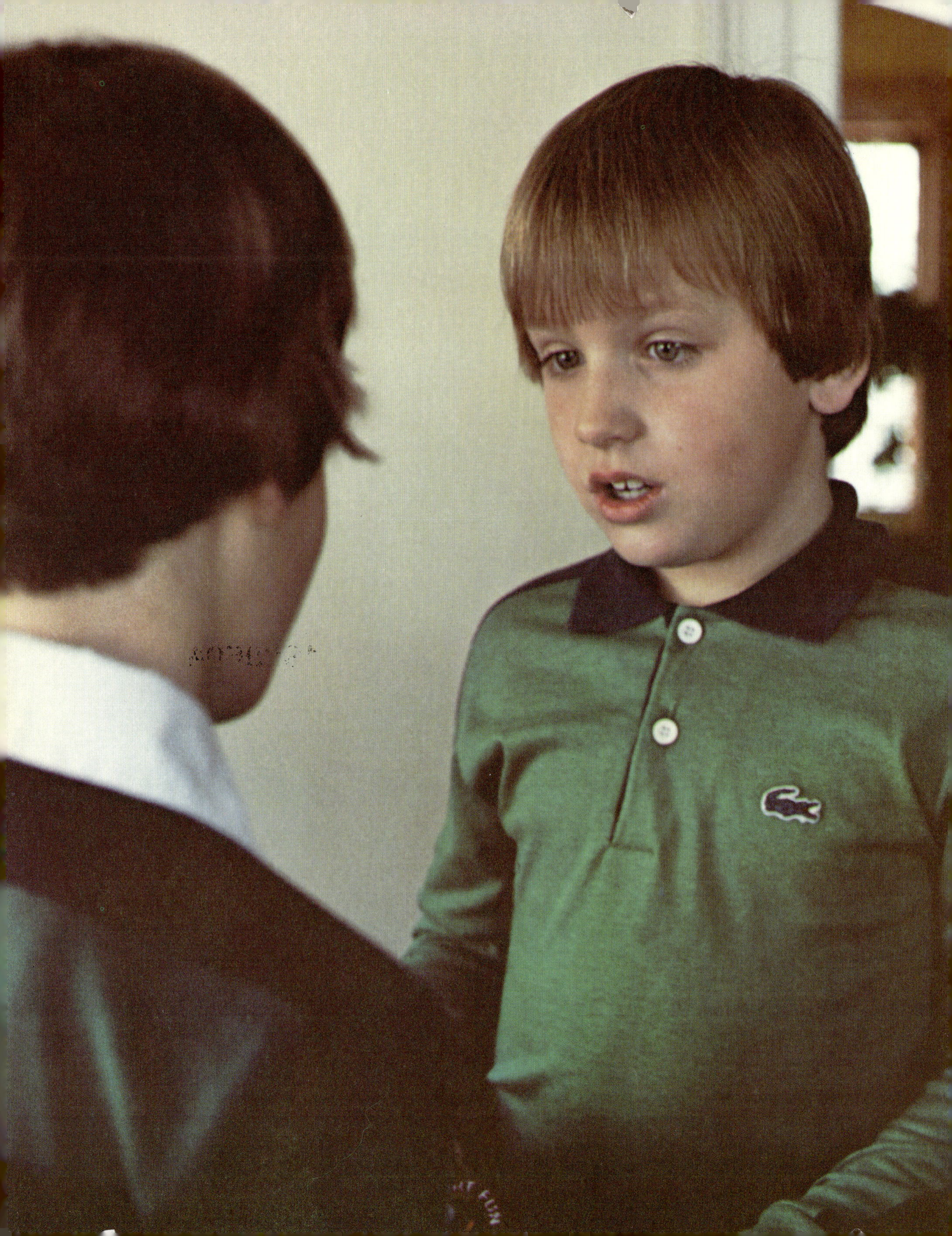

"Wait a minute, Barry," I said. "Don't get mad. I still want to be friends. I know you were just trying to help me out. But stealing isn't doing something nice for a friend. It's wrong. Besides, you could have been in big trouble. Those wheels are worth a lot of money."

Barry looked angry. "Do you think I would have lifted them if I thought I could get caught?" he said. "They were having a meeting or something in the back of the store. Nobody saw me."

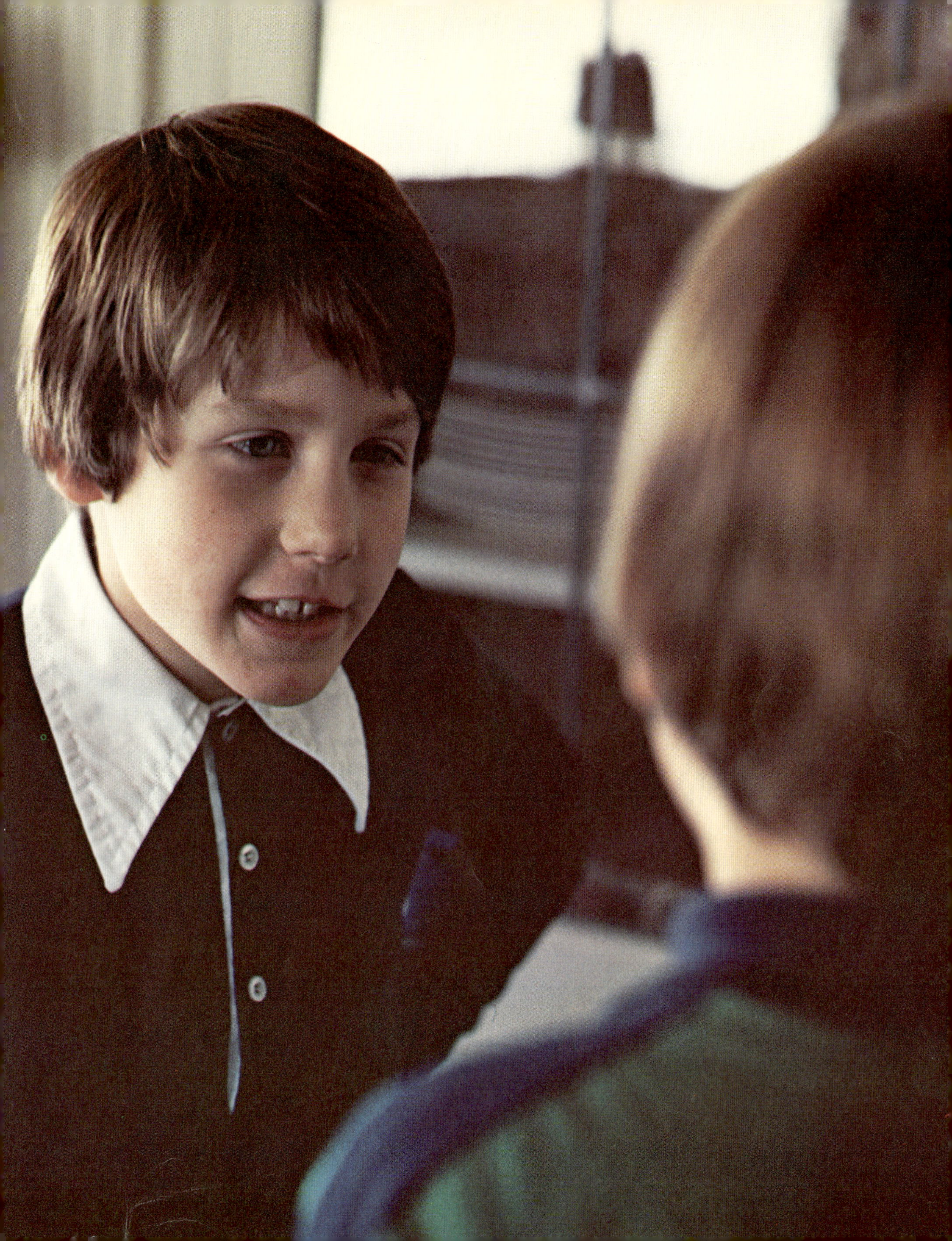

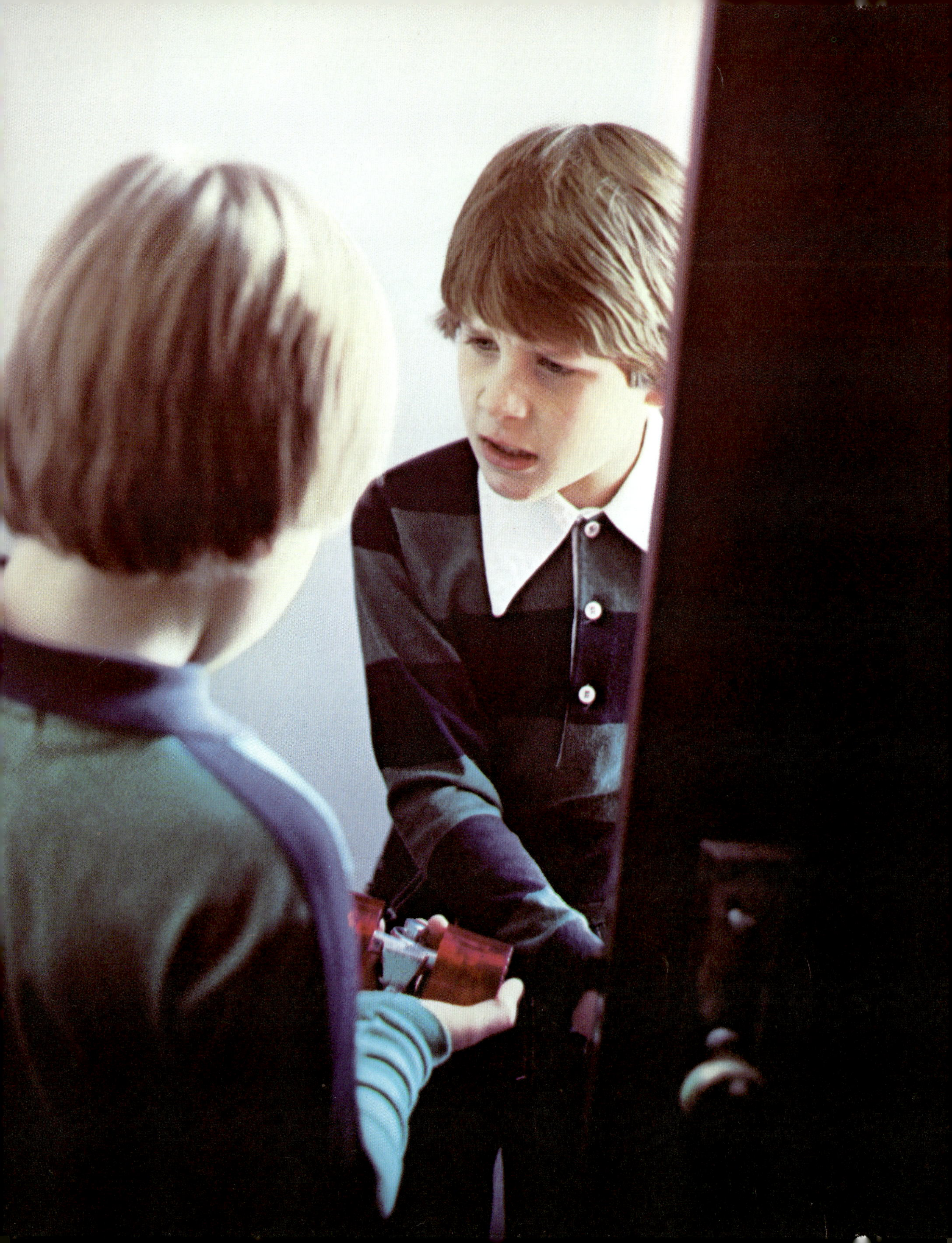

"Well, what about me?" I asked. "What if my parents ask where I got the wheels?"

Barry laughed. "Are you kidding?" he said. "They probably won't even notice. If they say anything, just tell them you finally washed enough cars to pay for them."

"My parents would know that's a lie. Then they'd really be mad," I said.

Barry got up and walked to the door. "I'm getting out of here," he said. "You're such a goody-goody. I'm leaving."

"Okay, go ahead. But take these with you," I said and handed him the wheels. "I don't want them."

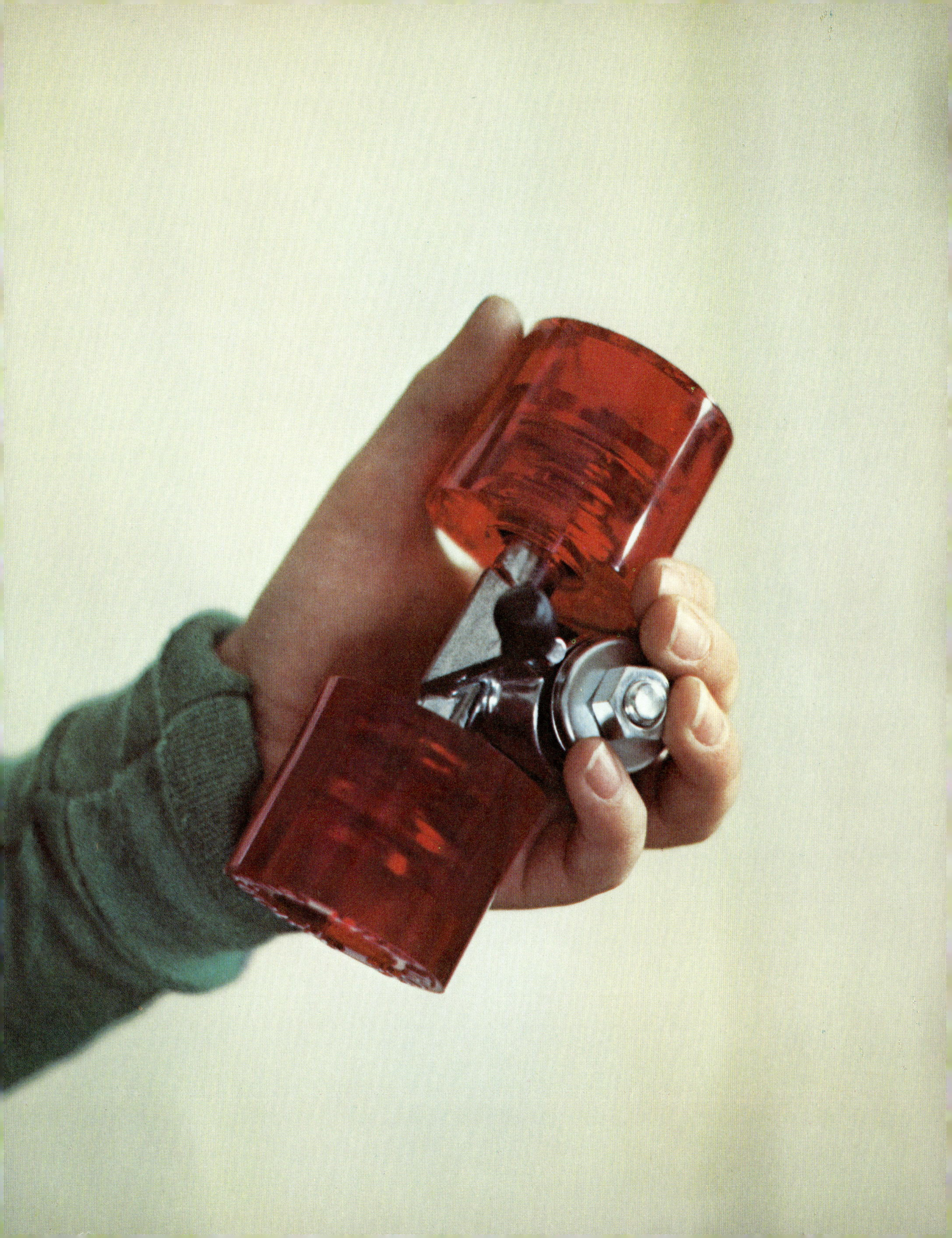